DON'T PA

The lead-up to exa... panic! When we fe... God slip down ou... can become optio... Christians, we se... glorify Him. We should fit our revision in around living for God, and not squeeze God into spare moments. We all need encouragement sometimes, so we've written **Don't Panic!** to encourage you to keep your eyes fixed on God as you revise.

Through reading the Bible, God can encourage us, strengthen us and prepare us to serve Him even when we're revising. And by talking to Him regularly in prayer, we can praise God, share with Him what's on our minds, and ask for His help. But don't forget: it's still important to work hard! Being a Christian is no guarantee to passing our exams — even Christians fail sometimes! We can think that handing everything over to God means He'll help us pass, without us putting in the effort. But we need to work hard for God, so that He gets glory through our achievements and efforts.

Use **Don't Panic!** to aid your revision so that the Lord remains your number one focus through this busy time. With God on your side, you don't need to panic!

Contents

DON'T PANIC! was written by Martin Cole and Andrew Roycroft, with article ideas pilfered from Helen Thorne and Kirsty Cole, and lovely designery stuff by Steve Devane.

Revision timetable

WEEK 1

	MONDAY	TUESDAY	WEDNESDAY
9am			
10am			
11am			
12pm			
1pm			
2pm			
3pm			
4pm			
5pm			
6pm			
7pm			
8pm			
9pm			

WEEKEND BIBLE READING SUGGESTIONS

Saturday: Philippians 4 v 4-9

Sunday: Proverbs 3 v 5-10

Why not take Sunday off and have a rest from revision!
Set aside some extra time to pray and delve into the Bible.

Trust in the LORD with all your heart and do not lean on your own understanding. (Proverbs 3 v 5)

THURSDAY	FRIDAY	SATURDAY	SUNDAY

Prayer diary

Under each day, write down... **1.** Things to thank God for
2. Other people you can pray for **3.** Your own requests

Monday

Tuesday

Wednesday

Thursday

Friday

Saturday

Sunday

Oh Lord, let your ear be attentive to the
prayer of this your servant.
(NEHEMIAH 1 v 11)

4

Day 1 – Stressing: a point

Nehemiah 1 v 1-11

How are you feeling about your exams? Under pressure or
calm and relaxed? Nehemiah knew pressure. He had been
forcibly taken with many other Jews to the kingdom of
Persia. This was a heartbreaking experience for him, and
for anyone who truly loved God. Nehemiah also had a very
stressful job. He was responsible for making sure that the
king received only the best wine, and that it contained no
poison. One mistake, and Nehemiah's life could have been
over. Talk about stress!

Read Nehemiah 1 v 1-11
- **What upset Nehemiah so much (v3)?**
- **What was Nehemiah's reaction to this news (v4)?**

Nehemiah was devastated. More than anything, Nehemiah
was concerned for God's honour now that God's city of
Jerusalem lay in ruins. Even during exam season, God's
honour and people hearing the gospel should be our
priority too.

What could Nehemiah do in this situation? Verses 4-11
give us the answer – he turned to God. He set aside time
to pray and was open and honest before God, confessing
his sins, and then seeking the Lord's help. Verse 11 sees
Nehemiah cry out to the Lord, asking Him to intervene
and do the impossible.

SO WHAT?
As we face exams, we can feel overwhelmed by the task
that lies in front of us. It's easy to look at a crammed file
of notes and wonder how we'll ever be able to memorise it
all. We need help, but rarely think of turning to God for it!

PRAY!
Why not set aside ten or fifteen minutes at the start of
your day, or just before you begin revising, and talk to
God? Like Nehemiah, come before God and ask Him to
deal with anything that might spoil your relationship with
Him. And then simply pour your heart out to Him. God
will listen to you and answer your prayers!

Day 2 – Bullet-point prayers

Nehemiah 2 v 1-6

A million thoughts rush through your head. Have I got everything I need? Where did I put my notes? I'm late!! In the middle of exam day madness, it's easy to feel helpless and have that nagging feeling that you haven't prepared or prayed enough.

Read Nehemiah 2 v 1-3

☑ **Do you bottle up your emotions or let them show?**
☑ **How did Nehemiah respond to the king's question (v2-3)?**
☑ **How honest are you when people ask 'How's it going?'**

Sometimes, as Christians, we think that we must always be smiley, never showing our anxiety. Nehemiah blows this out of the water. He just can't hide his feelings anymore. He's upset about God's city, Jerusalem, being in ruins, and the king notices. Nehemiah 2 v 1-2 show us that it's okay to admit to the world that we feel low and that we find life hard sometimes.

Read verses 4-6

☑ **What did Nehemiah instinctively do when faced with the king's blunt question (v4)?**

Between the king's question and Nehemiah's answer, Nehemiah **'prayed to the God of heaven'**. Nice one! In a split second, Nehemiah breathed a simple, sincere prayer to God, instinctively seeking God's help in a tight spot. And God answered (v6).

SO WHAT?

Through His death and resurrection, Jesus has made it possible for Christians to approach God with the ordinary things in our lives. In your exams, make it your practice to simply breathe out split-second bullet-point prayers to God.

It's a prayer reflex. When a problem comes, we should instantly and automatically share it with God. It's a wonderful feeling, in the middle of an exam or revision, to simply cry to the God of heaven, and know that He hears and will answer even the briefest of prayers.

Day 3 – Don't worry, be happy

Matthew 6 v 25-34

Before you do any more revision, take a walk outside,
breathe in the fresh air and look around. Go on, give it a
go, and take this book and your Bible with you if it's not
raining. Can you see or hear any birds? It's OK, we're not
investigating the biblical principles of bird-watching, or
suggesting you hug a tree – we're setting the scene for
Jesus' teaching.

Read Matthew 6 v 25-30
▢ **What simple point is Jesus making here?**
Looking at birds, we can see the infinite care and intimate
knowledge that God has of them, and how He supplies
their every need. Now for a bit of multiplication. If God
provides for such small and insignificant creatures, how
much more effort and love will He show to you, who He
has loved enough to send His own Son to die for!

Read verses 31-34
▢ **Which of Jesus' sentences strikes you the most?**
▢ **How do you need to apply Jesus' words to your life?**
▢ **How do we go about seeking God's kingdom?**
It's so easy to get caught up in life, and with the worries
and wants of the world around us. But Jesus tells us not
to chase those things, but to seek God's kingdom: actively
leading people to know Jesus as their King. And to seek
His righteousness: making it our ambition to live His way.

SO WHAT?

How can you apply v33 to your own life?

PRAY!
▢ **What needs of yours can God meet right now?**
Talk to the Lord about these things and ask Him to help
you seek His kingdom and His righteousness. Trust Him
that the other stuff will fall into place.

Day 4 – Feeling sheepish

Psalm 23

Grab a scrap of paper and write down some of the things that are weighing on your mind at the moment. Yesterday we were encouraged by Jesus not to worry. But it's not an easy thing to master, is it? Today, David gives us some great reasons why we don't need to worry.

Read Psalm 23 v 1-3
- **What did it mean for David to have the Lord as his shepherd (v1-3)?**

Are you encouraged by those verses? God cares for, looks after and leads His sheep, Christians. He gives them everything they need (v1). He feeds them and gives them rest (v2). Jesus called Himself the **good shepherd** (John 10 v 11), and in His death and resurrection, met our needs for forgiveness, purpose in life and hope for the future.
- **How does Jesus restore your soul (v3)?**
- **How does He guide you in the paths of right living?**

Read verses 4-6

God is with us through the tough times: guiding us, comforting us. Whether it's exam stress, relationship troubles or even facing death (v4), Christians can be confident because the Lord is with them every step of the way.

SO WHAT?

The Lord is with us in the good times (v1-3) and the bad (v4). Verses 5 and 6 point us to eternal life and the secure future we have because of Jesus. We don't really need to worry because our future is safe in the Lord and we will live in His house forever (v6)!

PRAY!

Thank God for His amazing, ongoing, personal care. And thank Him for Jesus, the Good Shepherd. Ask Him to help you know He's with you through the tough times, and to help you call out to Him for guidance as you prepare for exams.

Tomorrow, we'll think more about having a rest...

Day 5 – Have a break...

Mark 6 v 30-34

A TV programme called *Shattered* offered a large cash prize to anyone who could stay awake for an entire week. As contestants became more and more tired, their faces began to look worn, their speech became slurred, their minds became paranoid and hallucinogenic, and their bodies began to progressively shut down. Without exception, every single one of us needs to rest. Jesus recognised this too...

Read Mark 6 v 30-34

- **How did Jesus show His care for His disciples (v30-31)?**
- **How else did Jesus show His compassion (v34)?**

Jesus' disciples had just returned from preaching in Galilee. Life had become so hectic that they didn't even have time to eat (v31). So Jesus told them to go with Him somewhere quiet and chill out for a bit (v31). He understood the pressures they were under and ordered them to get some rest.

SO WHAT?

Human beings need rest and relaxation. At the moment you're probably working long hours, and living life at a fairly frantic pace. If that's the case, take a break and give your body and mind a chance to recuperate.

Such advice might sound impossible to you right now. But the Lord didn't tell His disciples to wait until a quiet period and then get some rest. When the battle was at its fiercest, He told them to relax. Only you can decide to take a break, and give yourself a chance to get some rest.

The disciples' break was short lived – in v33 we see a frantic mob waiting for them. Jesus showed compassion to them by **teaching** them! We need to take a break sometimes. But we also need to keep learning from Jesus. Don't let exams get in the way of Bible study. Maybe you can combine a time of relaxation with feeding yourself from God's word.

For suggestions for weekend Bible readings, see the revision timetable.

How to revise

Revision means to look at something again and refresh your knowledge. The basic assumption is that you've already studied the material. Hopefully, you shouldn't be coming across any new ideas, or anything you can't understand, and you might find you can already remember a good percentage of the material. So revision isn't that difficult. Honest. But it is hard work, because it involves training your mind to remember things. Plus there is the scary factor of having an exam just round the corner.

Revision plan

Not having a revision plan is a bit like not having a shopping list – you're bound to forget something, and it will probably be vital. Time spent on a revision plan is time well spent. Work out how much time you have available for revision, and assign a slot to each topic or unit. Make sure you revise everything at some stage, and try to revise topics more than once, as this will help them stay in your memory better. Leave room for some flexibility as your revision progresses, but try to stick to your plan. You might find the weekly revision timetables we've printed useful.

How do I begin?

Find somewhere quiet to revise, set aside a good block of time and get down to it!

Take a small section and revise for 5-10 minutes by taking notes, drawing a diagram, making a list of key words or ideas, or whatever you find most helpful. Then test yourself, either by answering a specific question or by writing down what you can remember. When you're satisfied, be confident and move on to the next section. Once you've been going for a while, you'll quickly identify those areas that require most study, as well as those you feel weakest in. Don't forget to allow extra time for brushing up on these in your revision plan.

Revision technique

Everybody has their own learning style, so you might not find all of these ideas helpful. Try picking three or four:

- copy out the key points from each unit onto index cards and carry them with you to re-read in spare moments
- record your notes onto a cassette/dictaphone/MP3 player so you can play them back to yourself whenever you like
- write out key facts and vocabulary and ask a friend to test you
- write important words or phrases onto sticky notes and stick them in prominent places (beside the kettle, on the bathroom mirror, around your computer monitor, on your CD collection, by the loo, but please not on the inside of the car windscreen)
- use diagrams or pictures – draw your own to help you remember them more effectively
- write an A4 summary, get it laminated, stick it above the taps and read it while enjoying a good relaxing bath
- if you use public transport, never underestimate the revision potential of a delayed bus or train.

Practising for the exam

As well as revising your notes, you need to make sure you know what will be required of you in the exam. Have a go at answering questions from sample papers. Allow yourself the amount of time you'll have in the exam, and answer the questions as well as you can. Then review them yourself – what was good? What could be better? What gaps are there in your knowledge? Where and how do you need to improve? You could even get someone to give you feedback on the questions you attempted.

The last 24 hours before the exam

The temptation is to build up towards a revision frenzy in the final few hours before the exam. But while you may have been able to get away with studying all night in the past, it's far more sensible to make sure you go into the exam with a clear head and a lively mind! There's a lot to be said for getting a good night's sleep before the exam. And don't forget breakfast – the exam will seem incredibly long if you start to feel peckish after the first 15 minutes! Beyond that, turn up in plenty of time with all the materials you'll need, take a spare pen, relax and try to enjoy the exam...

Revision timetable

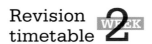

	MONDAY	TUESDAY	WEDNESDAY
9am			
10am			
11am			
12pm			
1pm			
2pm			
3pm			
4pm			
5pm			
6pm			
7pm			
8pm			
9pm			

WEEKEND BIBLE READING SUGGESTIONS

Saturday: Colossians 3 v 1-11

Sunday: Colossians 3 v 12-17

Why not take Sunday off and have a rest from revision!
Set aside some extra time to pray and delve into the Bible.

Each one should use whatever gift he has received to serve others, faithfully administering God's grace in its various forms. (1 Peter 4 v 10)

THURSDAY	FRIDAY	SATURDAY	SUNDAY

Prayer diary

Under each day, write down... **1.** Things to thank God for
2. Other people you can pray for **3.** Your own requests

Monday

Tuesday

Wednesday

Thursday

Friday

Saturday

Sunday

Be clear minded and self-controlled so that
you can pray.
(1 PETER 4 v 7)

Day 6 – Weird living

1 Peter 4 v 1-6

The lads I lived with at uni were not Christians. This was pretty evident in their language and their pursuit of a good time. It really got me down when I realised that my life often wasn't very different from theirs. But I remember one of my housemates saying to me "You don't swear like the rest of us – good for you". I was gobsmacked! Somehow, my attempt to live a God-honouring life did have an effect on my friends.

It's a constant battle trying to live as a Christian in an ungodly world. This week, we're dipping into 1 Peter, which is all about the tough times we face as Christians. It's loaded with practical advice on honouring Jesus with the way we live.

Read 1 Peter 4 v 1-6

- How do 'pagans' (non-Christians) live (v3)?
- Why should we not live the same way (v1-2)?
- How does the world view the way Christians live (v4)?

Jesus Christ suffered on the cross (v1) to die on our behalf and rescue us from the punishment we deserve for our sin (1 Peter 3 v 18). So we must also be prepared to suffer as we aim to live like Jesus (v1). That means giving up our old sinful desires (v2), our friends thinking we're weird for doing this and giving us a hard time for it (v4). Jesus wants us to have His attitude towards sin. And one day Jesus will judge everyone fairly (v5).

SO WHAT?

Do non-believers around you think you're strange for the way you live, or do you have an easy ride because you're exactly the same as them? What things from your sinful past do you need to throw out of your Christian life?

PRAY!

It's time to do business with God. Be brutally honest about the specific areas of your life you haven't fully given over to Him. Ask the Lord to help you beat these sins. Ask Him to help you stand out as His servant among your friends.

Tomorrow, we'll put all of this into practice...

Day 7 – Getting your hands dirty

1 Peter 4 v 7-11

In A-level Law I learned the principles behind the judicial system and the specifics of criminal law, such as the law on theft. But if I was suddenly thrown into court and told to prosecute someone for grand theft, I'd be hopeless – I wouldn't know where to start! It's one thing knowing the **theory**, it's something else entirely to **put it into practice**. Yesterday, Peter taught us the theory of living as Christ's followers in an ungodly world. Today, he gives us practical advice on how to actually do it.

Read 1 Peter 4 v 7
- **What two characteristics are important in believers?**
- **Why is it hard to pray when our minds are not clear?**

The world is moving towards its end, when Jesus will return. Keeping that in mind, we need to get stuck into serving Him. That means being clear-minded about the way we live, showing self-control when it comes to sin and throwing ourselves into prayer. And that's just for starters...

Read verses 8-11
- **In what practical ways can we show our love (v9-10)?**
- **What gifts/abilities has God given you (don't say none!)?**
- **What things should our gifts be used for (v10-11)?**

Love isn't all mushy and huggy, it's about serving people (v10), helping them out, inviting them round your place (v9), and being gracious – giving to others without expecting anything back (v10).

SO WHAT?

It sounds like hard work. Well it is, but God will give us the strength we need and Jesus will be praised when we serve others (v11)! You know the theory, now put it into practice. Make an encouraging phone call... test your friends on their subjects...

PRAY!

Read today's verses again. What has really challenged you? Talk to God about it. And thank God for giving us the abilities and strength to live for Him, serving others.

Day 8 – Celebrate suffering!

1 Peter 4 v 12-19

Has anything like this ever happened to you? You had
the opportunity to mention that you're a Christian
and you chickened out. Or maybe you told friends that
praying helps you cope with revision and they laughed
in your face. Or perhaps you stuck up for the Bible in a
conversation and soon you were on the receiving end of
some very passionate arguments. Peter says that if you're
a Christian, you should expect to suffer...

Read 1 Peter 4 v 12-14
- **Is it unusual to suffer as a Christian (v12)?**
- **Why should we be happy to suffer for Christ
(v13, 14)?**

Tough times and ridicule are a pain in the neck, but Peter
says *get used to it!* Jesus suffered to rescue us and we'll
share in that suffering. But Jesus' suffering was followed
by glory, when He was raised back to life and went to rule
with His Father God. One day we'll share in that glory
too (v14)!

Read verses 15-19
- **Why else is it a privilege to suffer as a Christian
(v16)?**

It's an amazing honour to be called a Christian – carrying
Jesus Christ's name (v16). And if you think life is hard
as a Christian, think how much worse it will be for those
who go against God and reject Jesus (v17-18). One day
they'll face God's judgment.

SO WHAT?

Think back to the examples I mentioned at the beginning.
How could this passage help you out when you face hassle
for your faith? Peter says don't be surprised if you suffer
as a Christian. In fact, it's a reason to celebrate!

PRAY!

Exams aren't suffering for God, but being prepared to stand
out from the crowd can lead to suffering in Jesus' name.
Thank God that you carry Jesus' name and will share in His
glory. Ask God's help in standing up as a follower of Christ.
God can give you the strength and courage to cope with any
hassle or suffering that comes your way.

Day 9 – Cast away

1 Peter 5 v 1-7

Are you a sheep or a shepherd? A born leader or happy to be behind the scenes? Whichever you are, Peter has something to say to you...

Read 1 Peter 5 v 1-4

Peter is speaking particularly to leaders in the church (youth group and C.U. count, so listen up).

☑ **How should Christians who have responsibility act (v2-3)?**

Peter gives clear guidelines for Christian leaders – look after those in your care. That means serving them, not bossing them about (v3). It's not about what you can get out of it, but what you can give to other believers. Jesus, the *Chief Shepherd*, will reward those who have served Him when He returns (v4).

Read verses 5-6

☑ **What should our attitude be to older Christians (v5)?**

Do you find it hard to take orders or advice from other people? I do! But Peter says be humble, swallow your pride, listen to older Christians, put others first.

• **In which of your relationships do you need to work at showing more humility?**

Read verse 7

What's on your mind right now? You can hand it over to God! He wants to take your worries off your hands, because He cares for you. Sometimes it's hard to believe that our all-powerful God would care for anyone as puny, sinful and insignificant as us. But He does! Learn verse 7 off by heart or write it out and stick it where you'll see it; it's important to hold on to.

PRAY!

Ask God to help you serve Him in your relationships. Not to lord it over people, but to serve other believers. To be humble. To respect your elders. Now tell God what worries are weighing on your mind and ask Him to help you with those issues.

Day 10 – Beware of the lion

1 Peter 5 v 8-11

What's your instant reaction when you see a BEWARE OF THE DOG sign on a gate? Mild terror? Well, get ready for a bigger scare. Today, Peter sticks a large BEWARE OF THE LION sign right in front of our eyes. Sounds pretty serious...

Read 1 Peter 5 v 8-11
- **How can we avoid this lion taking us by surprise (v8)?**
- **What must we do when we spot him (v9)?**
- **Why can we be confident against such a terrifying enemy (v10)?**

Peter describes the devil as a lion looking for someone to devour. As you face exams, you're under all kinds of strain — mental exhaustion, physical tiredness, emotions all over the place. Your enemy Satan knows the stress that you're going through at the moment. He knows how vulnerable you are as you work long hours, and like a roaring lion, he will be roaming about looking for ways to obstruct you in your walk with God.

SO WHAT?

Peter says be on your guard, keeping self-control (v8). He tells us that the best way to resist the devil is by *'standing firm in the faith'* (v9). That means not getting distracted by all our concerns and worries, but keeping our eyes focused on serving God and honouring Him in the way we live. Satan will try to undermine your relationship with God, making you feel too sinful or unimportant for God to love you. Or maybe he'll make you doubt that you're really a Christian.

PRAY!

Today, beware of the lion. Recognise the negative thoughts the devil puts in your mind. And ask God to help you resist these feelings and know the certainty of His love and grace. Keep talking to God! Continually praise God throughout the day for His love, and ask for His help. Peter reminds his readers in v9 that they are not the only people to face these problems – all of God's people face this kind of opposition. Take a few moments now to ask God to protect you and other Christians who are facing testing times.

Coping with stress

Help!

When people say *"I'm stressed!"* they can mean different things. Broadly speaking, we mean something along the lines of *'I've got too much to do and too little time to do it and I'm not sure I'm up to it and it's all weighing heavily on my mind and my body and... AAAAAARRRGGHHHHH!!!'*.

We can let stress overwhelm us. But we don't have to! The Bible gives us a godly, eternal perspective on our lives and our worries. It helps us to line up our priorities with God's and not with the expectations of ourselves and others.

Priority picking

It's worth asking yourself if your priorities are the same as God's. Maybe you're worried about getting good qualifications to ensure you do well in life and get a good job and earn enough money. But the Bible says that God is our provider, and ultimately we need to recognise that we are dependent on Him, not on ourselves.

'Seek first his kingdom and his righteousness, and all these things will be given to you as well' (Matthew 6 v 33).
Getting our priorities straight means putting God first; realising that our exams and our achievements are not the be all and end all. The gospel comes first. Always. Serving God, making sure we give Him our time, telling others about Jesus – these things must get priority. Let's face it, our worries and stresses really aren't as important!

Identity crisis

Sometimes we can think we need to do well academically to gain fulfilment in life. Our self-worth can rest on it. But the Bible is clear that God's purposes for us are most important, and that it is only through knowing God and serving Him that we fulfil His purpose for our lives. Jesus said: 'I have come that they may have life, and have it to the full' (John 10 v 10). Our identity is in Jesus, not in exam results or the job we end up with.

Great expectations

Some of the stress in our lives can come from a desire to please other people; to live up to the expectations of our parents, teachers, tutors or peers. 'My dad has paid for my education – it will be so disappointing to him if I don't finish top of the class.' 'I got a 'B' last time, so I'm expected to do at least as well again this time.'

This truth is obvious but rarely applied: **other people don't matter more than God**. God doesn't expect us to do more than we can realistically do! If we're pushing ourselves too hard, we're probably trying to meet others' expectations, not God's.

'Fear of man will prove to be a snare, but whoever trusts in the LORD is kept safe.' (Proverbs 29 v 25) For Christians, God alone is our Master. Do your best and work your hardest to serve Him. Don't get yourself in a state because of others' expectations.

Treasure hunting

We need to remind ourselves that this life will not last for ever and is not all there is. What a relief! If we know Jesus, we have an eternity with Him to look forward to. During exams, as at any other time, our priority should be serving Him and working for things that are going to last. Jesus said: *'Store up for yourselves treasures in heaven, where moth and rust do not destroy, and where thieves do not break in and steal. For where your treasure is, there your heart will be also'* (Matthew 6 v 20-21).

Talk talk

It's one thing reading what the Bible says about stress, but it can be a struggle to put it into practice. The best thing you can do is talk to your heavenly Father. Tell Him about your plans for each day, about how you're feeling and what you're worried about. Ask God to show you His priorities and give you the strength you need to serve Him. Hand your stress over to God. *'Cast all your anxiety on him for he cares for you'* (1 Peter 5 v 7).

Revision timetable

WEEK 3

	MONDAY	TUESDAY	WEDNESDAY
9am			
10am			
11am			
12pm			
1pm			
2pm			
3pm			
4pm			
5pm			
6pm			
7pm			
8pm			
9pm			

WEEKEND BIBLE READING SUGGESTIONS

Saturday: Psalm 111

Sunday: Psalm 113

Why not take Sunday off and have a rest from revision!
Set aside some extra time to pray and delve into the Bible.

Whatever you do, work at it with all your heart, as working for the Lord, not for men.
(Colossians 3 v 23)

THURSDAY	FRIDAY	SATURDAY	SUNDAY

Prayer diary

Under each day, write down... **1.** Things to thank God for
2. Other people you can pray for **3.** Your own requests

Monday

Tuesday

Wednesday

Thursday

Friday

Saturday

Sunday

I waited patiently for the LORD; he turned
to me and heard my cry.
(PSALM 40 v 1)

Day 11 – Who's the boss?

Colossians 3 v 18-25

The Bible has loads of practical advice for living as God's children – Christians – in an ungodly world. This week we're going to unpack some of this teaching and apply it to our lives as we prepare for exams.

One of the worst jobs I took as a student was putting the tops on talcum powder bottles. The factory seemed to have a huge chain of command with me at the very bottom. This gave various people the chance to lord it over us lowly students. But when you're studying for exams, you only have yourself to answer to. You have no boss, right? Well, not exactly...

Read Colossians 3 v 18-22
☑ **Any ideas what this has got to do with revising???**
Check out the last few words of verses 18, 20 and 22. These verses describe different relationships; in all of these relationships, the writer Paul says **do what pleases the Lord**. Ultimately we answer to God and should be seeking to please Him in our relationships with other people.

Read verses 23-25
☑ **What should be our attitude towards work (v23)?**
☑ **Are you really your own boss?**
As Christians, we answer to God. So when we work (and that includes studying!) we should give our all to it, because we're doing it for God (v23). Are you studying for yourself, to please your parents, or just because it's what you have to do? For Christians, work is not just work, it's serving God. It's a way of showing our gratitude for everything He's done for us and everything we'll receive in eternity (v24).
☑ **How will this change the way you work today?**

PRAY!
Thank God that He is the boss of your life. Thank Him for everything He has done for you. Ask the Lord to give you a new enthusiasm for your work and revision. Ask Him to keep reminding you that it's Him you're serving in everything you do.

Day 12 – Bitesize revision

Exodus 18

More biblical, practical advice today. Sometimes there just aren't enough hours in the day to get everything done. Even Moses had that problem!

Let's set the scene: Jethro is visiting his son-in-law, Moses. He was thrilled when he heard how the Lord had spectacularly rescued the Israelites from slavery in Egypt (v9). Jethro became convinced that God was the one true God and worth living for (v11)! Next, Jethro followed Moses around in his daily duties...

Read **Exodus 18 v 13-27**
- **How would you describe Moses' day?**
- **What was Jethro's advice (v17-23)?**

To say that Moses was a busy man is a huge understatement (v13). Jethro had the advantage of being an impartial observer, and he realised that Moses' workload was too much for any man to handle. Jethro advised Moses to split the people into groups and appoint different men to look after groups of thousands, hundreds, fifties, and tens. That way the work would still get done, and Moses would be 'able to stand the strain' (v23).

SO WHAT?

Are you trying to do too much? How can you break up your work and revision into realistic, manageable chunks? What responsibilities can you hand over to others? How can you help over-stretched Christian workers? Like Jethro, older and wiser believers can help make sense of the madness in our lives. Which older Christian can you confide in and perhaps study the Bible with?

PRAY!

Ask God to help you make wise and realistic decisions about your use of time and how you can best serve Him. And ask Him to give you someone you can confide in, who can give you wise, godly advice.

Day 13 – In the mood

Psalm 40

The time leading up to exams can be an emotional one, with our feelings jumping all over the place. In Psalm 40, we see David's mood change as he talks honestly to God.

Read Psalm 40 v 1-5

🔲 **What was David's past experience of God (v1-2)?**

It's easy to get caught up in the moment, worrying about what is happening now – our busy day, things on our minds, revision we haven't done. In this psalm, David remembers God's grace and rescue in the past. And he recognises that God has a plan for his life (v5). As the craziness of our lives seems to spiral out of control, we can remember how God has been faithful to us before, and see His plan for us unfolding. God is in control – He has helped us in the past and He's completely faithful.

Read verses 6-10

🔲 **How would you describe David's mood in these verses?**

🔲 **What was David's response to God's faithfulness (v8-10)?**

When we recognise God's hand at work in our lives, our desire should be one of dedication to Him in everything we do (v8). Do you let other people know the impact God has had on your life (v9-10)? Or do you keep quiet and take the praise for yourself?

🔲 **Who do you need to be more honest with about God's work in your life?**

Read verses 11-17

Finally, David opens up about how he feels right now – he feels rotten about his sin and overwhelmed with troubles. Maybe you can identify with him a little. But he doesn't wallow in self-pity; he hands it over to God and asks God to rescue him.

PRAY!

Try David's prayer pattern…

1. Thank God for specific things He has done for you in the past.
2. Ask God to help you serve Him more and have the courage to tell others about His impact on your life.
3. Tell God what's on your mind and plead with Him to help you.

Day 14 – All talk

Proverbs

Blah blah blah. You probably have words coming out of your ears by now: endless revision notes your brain can no longer process; moans and whinges escaping from your lips; other people irritating you with how well or badly their exams are going. Too many words. The book of Proverbs has wise advice for us about the words we use every day.

Read **Proverbs 10 v 19, 13 v 3, 17 v 27-28**
- **What should be our attitude to our own words?**
- **How can our words lead to sin?**

When someone says something that puts us on edge, we want to rip into them and tell them what we think of them. But the Bible says **TIME OUT!** Hold your tongue or you'll regret it. In fact, keeping quiet is often the **wise** thing to do (10 v 19).

Read **Proverbs 12 v 18**
- **What can be the good and bad effects of our words?**
- **How have your words hurt someone recently?**

It's pretty obvious that our words can cause pain. But what we say can heal, soothe and comfort too! The right words can bring an end to arguments and bad feeling. They can comfort a friend at the end of their tether. Who will you comfort or encourage with your words today?

Read **Proverbs 27 v 17**

God can use conversation in a powerful way. Talking to other believers can help us to grow, sharpening each other as a blacksmith sharpens iron with iron. Why not arrange to meet with Christian friends for coffee and a chat, to encourage each other in your faith? Why not sit in a different seat than normal this Sunday, and talk to someone in church you've never spoken to before? It's good to talk — show someone you care today, and you'll be a sharper Christian as a result.

PRAY!

Time to **talk** to God...

Day 15 – It wasn't me!

Psalm 115

No matter what happened at school it was never anybody's fault. Whether it was shouting in the corridors or a broken window, every time a teacher arrived on the scene there'd be a chorus of voices saying *'It wasn't me'.* Of course, when compliments or prizes were being dished out, people were much quicker to own up and accept the praise.

How eager are we to pass on the credit to the One who really deserves it? The writer of Psalm 115 shows us the way...

Read Psalm 115 v 1-15
- **What does God do for His people (v9-15)?**
- **What should be our response to success (v1)?**

Psalm 115 was probably written when the work on God's temple in Jerusalem was completed. As everyone stood looking up at the finished work, they lifted their voices in chorus and sang: *'Not to us, O Lord...but to your name be the glory'* (v1). They knew that everything they had achieved as God's people wasn't down to them (or idols, v2-8) but was because of God's love and faithfulness (v1).

Read verses 16-18
- **What great privilege has God given us (v16)?**
- **Who should be praising God and telling people all that He's done (v17-18)?**

SO WHAT?

If you've known God's help and care over these past few weeks, then give Him all of the glory. When you speak with your friends about the stresses and strains of your exams, will you say: 'It wasn't me, God got me through it'? And when you receive your results, will you give it all back to God and glorify Him for His help and guidance? Whether your results are better or worse than you hoped, will you honour God's name for bringing you through and being constantly with you?

How to survive exams

The last 24 hours

Remember that it's normal to feel nervous before an exam!
It can even be a good sign that you're keyed up and ready
for the challenge. Some students try to combat their
nervousness with frenetic, non-stop cramming. This is
rarely successful.

It's far more helpful to make sure you arrive at the exam
in a position to do as well as possible with the revision
you've already done. Some top tips...

- **Try to get a good night's rest** before your exam day.
  Even if you're jangling with nerves, make sure you
  relax yourself rather than cram all night! You might
  find watching a favourite DVD or getting stuck into
  a novel will help take your mind off your exam.

- **Make sure you've eaten**—you don't want to be
  distracted by a rumbling stomach and thoughts of
  food during your exam.

- **Take time out for God.** This is something we so
  often drop on exam day. But what better preparation
  than being encouraged by God's awesome word and
  spending time in prayer? Give it a go!

Blindingly obvious check-list

Tick off the things in the list to give yourself
confidence that you're ready for the exam and haven't
forgotten anything.

In the week before the exam...

- do you know what the exam will involve?
- do you know where the exam is to be held?
- do you know when the exam will start?

On the day before the exam...

- do you have everything you need for the exam?
- do you have spare pens?
- have you allowed time to relax and sleep well?

On the day of the exam...

- eat well – enough to sustain your brain's efforts!
- spend time with God
- arrive in plenty of time (but not too early!)

Before the exam starts...

- is your chair comfortable and desk steady?
- pray a bullet-point prayer, committing your efforts to God

Get stuck in!

Read the exam paper carefully and plan your answers. There is always a temptation once the invigilator says: 'You may now begin' to plunge into answering questions with wild abandon. But take your time so you know exactly what is required of you, and so that you don't misread questions.

Take a moment to read the paper thoroughly, and if there are quotes or pieces of information you'll struggle to keep in mind once you begin writing, jot them down on spare paper. Take care to choose your questions on the basis of how well you can answer that specific question, rather than how well you know that topic generally.

After the exam

Try not to spend too long talking about the specifics of the exam or musing on how well you think you did. Such comparisons with other people can knock your confidence for further exams.

Take a moment to praise God: you've got through another paper, and God has been with you, helping you throughout the day. Maybe read the next section of *Don't Panic!* (if you haven't already) now that you have more time to read God's word.

Revision timetable

WEEK 4

	MONDAY	TUESDAY	WEDNESDAY
9am			
10am			
11am			
12pm			
1pm			
2pm			
3pm			
4pm			
5pm			
6pm			
7pm			
8pm			
9pm			

WEEKEND BIBLE READING SUGGESTIONS

Saturday: Revelation 21 v 1-7

Sunday: Psalm 19

Why not take Sunday off and have a rest from revision!
Set aside some extra time to pray and delve into the Bible.

The LORD is good to those whose hope is in him,
to the one who seeks him. (Lamentations 3 v 25)

THURSDAY	FRIDAY	SATURDAY	SUNDAY

Prayer diary

Under each day, write down... **1.** Things to thank God for
2. Other people you can pray for **3.** Your own requests

`Monday`

`Tuesday`

`Wednesday`

`Thursday`

`Friday`

`Saturday`

`Sunday`

Cast all your anxiety on him because he cares for you.
(1 PETER 5 v 7)

Day 16 – New every morning

Lamentations 3 v 19-32

Feeling jaded yet? This week, we're going to be encouraged to stick at it! In the space below, jot down how you're feeling about your revision and your exams. And how you feel about life in general.

Are you feeling positive? If so, Jeremiah gives us some great reasons to praise and thank our awesome God. And if you're feeling weighed down by life, Jeremiah has words of encouragement in the darkness.

Read Lamentations 3 v 19-32
- **What is Jeremiah's change in outlook from v19 to v21?**
- **What was it about God that restored his hope (v22-25)?**
- **What is the only way forward for him (v26-30)?**

Jeremiah and the Israelites were mourning over the destruction of Jerusalem by the Babylonians. But we can draw parallels with our own times of hardship. The God who comforted and strengthened the Israelites is the same God who is with us now. God's love and compassion will never fail us (v22, 32) and are with God's people every day (v23).

SO WHAT?

Yes, we'll have to face tough times in life – there's no escaping that (v27-30) but *'The Lord is good to those whose hope is in him'* (v25). We are **never** without hope. In fact, as God's children we have the **certain hope** of eternal life through Jesus Christ. We can get so bogged down in our everyday lives that we forget to fix our eyes on our eternal future with Jesus.

PRAY!

Thank God for the certain and eternal hope you have because of His Son Jesus. Ask Him to give you the right, eternal perspective as you face your exams and any other difficult situations you're going through.

Day 17 – Winging it

Isaiah 40 v 25-31

Do you feel like you're soaring through the sky or being dragged through the mud? To help our perspective, we're turning to Isaiah. God is speaking through Isaiah to the Israelites. They've turned away from God many times, so He's going to punish them. But He has promised that He will forgive them and bring them back to Himself! And yet they're still moaning!

Read Isaiah 40 v 25-27
- **What example of God's power are we shown (v25-26)?**
- **What was the Israelites' attitude towards God (v27)?**

For more evidence of God's greatness and awesome power, check out v12-24. The Israelites had seen again and again how powerful and loving God is, yet they still complained to Him (v27)! Crazy. Not only that, He was the all-powerful Creator of the Universe! How could they whinge at Almighty God?!

Read verses 28-31
- **What does v28 tell us about the Lord?**
- **What does God give His people (v29-31)?**

Can you identify with v30? Been feeling tired and weary recently? Have you stumbled or taken a fall? God says that even young people, whose bodies and minds are at the peak of fitness, get tired and feel like they can't go on.

SO WHAT?

When we feel exhausted or like we've fallen into a big pit, we can rely on God to give us the strength we need. If our hope is in the Lord, He'll renew our strength (v31). The Lord will carry us along and we'll soar like eagles! Awesome stuff. We need to stop relying on our own strength to get us through, and rely on our everlasting, all-powerful God.

PRAY!

Use verses 12-26 as you praise and thank God for who He is. Say sorry for times you've turned against Him and times you've relied on your own strength. Almighty God can renew your strength and give you the energy to serve Him!

Day 18 – Finished

John 19 v 16-30

Are you sick of exams and being reminded how important they are? Let's focus on something far far more important: Jesus and His death for us.

Read John 19 v 16-30

☑ **Take time out to think about what Jesus did and its impact on your life. Read through the verses as many times you need to.**
☑ **Grab a notebook and jot down any thoughts you have.**
☑ **Write down anything you want to say to God.**

When Jesus was on earth, He knew there were things He had to do before His life could end. He had to fulfil all of the Old Testament promises and prophecies about the Messiah, and He had to fulfil God's will by dying on the cross for our sins. The main point of Jesus' life was His death. In v30 we hear Him cry: 'It is finished!'. At that moment on the cross, Jesus knew that He had completed His mission. On the third day He rose again, showing that God was satisfied with His offering for sin. If you trust in Jesus' death in your place, taking the punishment you deserve, all your sins are forgiven. It is finished!

SO WHAT?

As you look ahead to your results, you'll feel some uncertainty. Have I done enough to pass? What do I do next? In a sense, you'll just have to wait and see. But if you're a Christian, the future is not uncertain. Because Jesus finished the work He had to do, you know that the future means an eternal life with Him. Perhaps, though, you've never accepted Jesus' offer of forgiveness. As you finish your exams, think about the work that Jesus finished, as He died on the cross. What a result it would be if today you admitted to Him that you're a sinner, and asked Him to save you through His finished work! Jesus has done His work—now it lies with us to trust Him.

PRAY!

Use the notes you made earlier to offer honest praise to God.
Tomorrow, we'll feel the pain... and learn to love it!

Day 19 – No pain, no gain

Romans 5 v 1-5

Yesterday, we fixed our focus on Jesus and His death and resurrection. In his letter to Christians in Rome, Paul tells believers that they are not merely passive observers of Jesus' suffering. They benefit from it eternally, and can expect to share in His suffering.

Read **Romans 5 v 1-5**
- **What do those who trust Jesus now have (v1)?**
- **What surprising thing can we get excited about (v3)?**
- **Why should we be happy to suffer (v3-5)?**

This is an awesome passage. It tells us in v1 of the great work that the Lord Jesus has done for us – He has given us peace with God. And we now receive far more from God than we could ever deserve. But Paul adds that problems are part and parcel of being a believer – *'we rejoice in our sufferings'* (v3).

SO WHAT?

Perhaps you know this only too well. Maybe the pressure that you've faced over recent days has caused you heartache and trouble. Paul tells us that we should see the difficulties of life as an opportunity to grow spiritually. God has a plan for our lives – it is a great plan – but it doesn't guarantee a life of ease and relaxation.

Instead, God allows us to face times of suffering which make us trust in Him more, and help us grow in spiritual character. *'Suffering produces perseverance; perseverance, character; and character, hope.'* God allows us to experience hard times so that we develop spiritual muscles, and are made more fit to serve Him.

And that really is something to celebrate, especially as we have the certain hope of sharing God's glory. And the Holy Spirit in us reminds us of God's overwhelming love for us (v5). The Christian life truly is a matter of 'no pain, no gain'. Let's look at our troubles as opportunities to learn and grow spiritually.

Day 20 – The ultimate test

1 Corinthians 3 v 10-17

A student was coming to the end of his time at university. Before graduation, his tutor invited him into his office for coffee and a chat. The conversation went like this...

Tutor:	'What do you plan to do now that you've finished college?'
Student:	'I plan to get a highly-paid job and buy myself a really nice sports car.'
Tutor:	'And then what?'
Student:	'Well, eventually I'll meet a pretty girl, buy a house, get married, and raise a family.'
Tutor:	'And then what?'
Student:	'I'll do my best to get early retirement and we'll enjoy our grandchildren.'
Tutor:	'And then what?
Student:	'And then, I guess, I'll eventually die.'

The tutor paused, looked the young man in the eye, and asked: 'And then what?'. The student gave no answer. His mind hadn't gone beyond getting through life, and doing the things he wanted. Death and eternity just weren't a part of his thinking.

Read 1 Corinthians 3 v 10-17

Paul encourages the Corinthian Christians to think beyond this life and into the next. He wants them to realise that in the chaos of life's pressures and activities, only one thing really matters – what we do for Jesus. By now you're well acquainted with exams and tests, but Paul points us towards the ultimate test – when the Lord Jesus will look at our lives and examine our service for Him.

SO WHAT?

Christians can be sure of eternal life (how great is that???) but they must also make sure that the work they do for God is of the highest quality, and for Jesus, serving Him.

How can you fix your eyes on eternal life with Jesus, working for Him, rather than just having a nice life now?

How do you survive???

Katie Cole is studying *Primary Education at Bishop Grosseteste College, Lincoln. We asked her about life as a Christian at university.*

❓ What do you find most stressful – exams or coursework? And why is that?

Coursework. It's even more prolonged pain than exams!!

❓ If you could have only one CD and one DVD with you on your desert island, what would they be?

Joni Mitchell and Forrest Gump

❓ What difference has being a Christian made to your student life?

Aiming to live my life out fully for Jesus inspires me to do my best in everything, including work and exams. But my relationship with God also means that I have a different perspective on life and my future, believing that ultimately my grades and career are in God's hands and He knows what's best for me.

❓ What challenges and encouragements have you experienced?

I think being a Christian student is a flippin' HUGE challenge! Most things that the student culture promotes contrast majorly with the way the Bible says we should live. There are constant temptations and areas to slip up in, but there are also loads of precious opportunities to stand out and share the difference that God has made in your life with fellow students.

A massive encouragement for me has been the way that churches welcome, support and kind of adopt us poor students. This is the church family in action! It's also awesome to get involved in CU, where a bunch of Christian students can not only support and build each other up, but also unite in sharing the gospel at uni. I've been totally overwhelmed by how open students are to hearing about and even accepting what Jesus has done for them. It's AWESOME!

? On exam day, how do you handle your nerves and stress?

I have a good old pray, read a psalm and have a cup of tea.

? Have you experienced disappointment with exam results?

Yeah, I fluffed my A-levels a little bit so didn't get into uni first time around.

? How did you cope with that?

It's hard on the old ego, but God put verses from Proverbs in my head, which both challenged and blessed me loads. It taught me that God is bigger than exam results.

? What's your strangest exam experience?

Er, I once raced through an exam and was the first to finish so that I could go watch my friend's important presentation...a bit stupid but I still passed!

? Have there been any instances when you've really felt God's help or guidance in your studies/exams?

I often have an amazing and unnatural peace during exams and deadlines, which I figure is totally God calming me down. He calmed storms on the sea so I guess a nervous student is easy!

? If you could give just one sentence of advice to people cramming for exams, what would it be?

Do your best (man I sound like my mum!), have plenty of caffeine and just give it over to God!

Mental floss

Try these puzzles as a break from your revision and a chance to exercise your brain muscles!

Each **Sudoku** has a unique solution that can be reached logically without guessing. Enter digits from 1 to 9 into the blank spaces. Every row must contain one of each digit. So must every column, as must every 3x3 square.

Easy

			3			5	7	
2	8	5						1
7		4		2				
6	2	3			5			8
5	1		8		2		3	4
4			7			1	2	5
				4		8		7
9						4	6	3
	4	1			3			

Medium

6			8	9		5		
					6	8		
		7			4		1	
				7		1	6	8
2			6	8	5			3
8	7	6		3				
	2		9			7		
	5		2					
		4		5	7			2

Hard

		8					3	5
		2		9			1	
				8	6		7	
			6	3				
	7		8		9		5	
				1	4			
	1		2	6				
	8			5		9		
6	2					7		

Brainteasers

1. Take the letters **ERGRO**. Put three letters in front of them, and the same three letters after to form a common English word.

2. What number gives the same result when it is added to 1.5 as when it is multiplied by 1.5?

3. Which of the following words is the odd-one-out?
IBIS   IBEX   ORYX   SIKA   ZEBU

4. Peter picked one pepper more than Paul. Pat picked one pepper more than Pam. Peter and Paul picked 10 more peppers than Pat and Pam. Peter, Paul, Pat and Pam picked 60 peppers. How many peppers did Peter pick?

5. Add the missing vowels to give six 6-letter names of countries.
CND   KWT   MLW   MXC   BLZ   PNM

6. There was an old woman who lived in a shoe, and the only food she had for her ten children was six potatoes. How did she make sure that each child had an equal share?

Revision timetable

	MONDAY	TUESDAY	WEDNESDAY
9am			
10am			
11am			
12pm			
1pm			
2pm			
3pm			
4pm			
5pm			
6pm			
7pm			
8pm			
9pm			

Those who hope in the Lord will renew their
strength. They will soar on wings like eagles.
(Isaiah 40 v 31)

THURSDAY	FRIDAY	SATURDAY	SUNDAY

Revision
timetable

	MONDAY	TUESDAY	WEDNESDAY
9am			
10am			
11am			
12pm			
1pm			
2pm			
3pm			
4pm			
5pm			
6pm			
7pm			
8pm			
9pm			

Since we have been justified through faith, we have peace with God through our Lord Jesus Christ. (Romans 5 v 1)

THURSDAY	FRIDAY	SATURDAY	SUNDAY

What now?

What's next for you? Anxiously awaiting your results? Moving on to a new stage in your life — a new course, finding a job? Continuing with your studies? Whatever is next for you, the important thing is that you are God's child whatever you do!

Check out 1 John 2 v 28 – 3 v 3

KEEP GOING!

We often put so much importance on what's next for us: a new course, a new job, a new relationship. But whatever we're doing, our focus should be on living for Jesus, serving Him, being ready for when He returns (v28).

CHILDISH BEHAVIOUR

As a Christian, you are God's child (v1)! Your identity is not found in the course you're on, the job you have or the image you create around yourself. First and foremost, you are God's child! God loves you so much that He calls you His son or daughter! Having this amazing privilege should spur us on to serving Him wherever we are and whatever we're doing.

FOCUS!

We have a certain hope that one day we will be with Jesus and we'll become even more like Him (v2). So let's fix our eyes on eternity with Jesus, living as His followers whatever our situation. Let's go for it!

FURTHER READING

Daily Bible notes — get plugged into your Bible every day. We'd like to recommend *Engage* for teenagers, and *Explore* if you're a bit older.

Hanging In There by John Dickson
Battles Christians Face by Vaughan Roberts
Guidance and the Voice of God by Jensen & Payne
The Busy Christian's Guide to Busyness by Tim Chester
All of these books can be found on the website
www.thegoodbook.co.uk